OUR BODY

Nervous System

Cheryl Jakab

Smart Apple Media

This edition first published in 2006 in the United States of America by Smart Apple Media.

Smart Apple Media
2140 Howard Drive West
North Mankato
Minnesota 56003

First published in 2006 by
MACMILLAN EDUCATION AUSTRALIA PTY LTD
627 Chapel Street, South Yarra, Australia 3141

Visit our Web site at www.macmillan.com.au

Associated companies and representatives throughout the world.

Library of Congress Cataloging-in-Publication Data

Jakab, Cheryl.
    The nervous system / by Cheryl Jakab.
    p. cm. — (Our body)
    Includes index.
    ISBN-13: 978-1-58340-735-6
    1. Nervous system—Juvenile literature. I. Title.

QP361.5 J35 2006
612.8—dc22   2005057886

Edited by Ruth Jelley
Text and cover design by Peter Shaw
Illustrations by Guy Holt, Jeff Lang (p. 4 (bottom), pp. 5–6),
    and Ann Likhovetsky (p. 30)
Photo research by Legend Images

Printed in USA

Acknowledgments
The author and the publisher are grateful to the following for permission to reproduce copyright material:

Front cover photograph: Colored SEM/scanning electron micrograph of human nerve cells, courtesy of Photolibrary/Steve Gschmeissner/Science Photo Library.
Front cover illustration by Jeff Lang.

VEM-BSIP/Auscape International, p. 22; The DW Stock Picture Library, pp. 21, 28; Photodisc, p. 13; Photolibrary/Botanica, p. 20; Photolibrary/Photo Researchers, Inc, p. 19; Photolibrary/Science Photo Library, pp. 7, 8, 12, 15, 16, 23, 24, 25, 26, 27, 29.

Contents

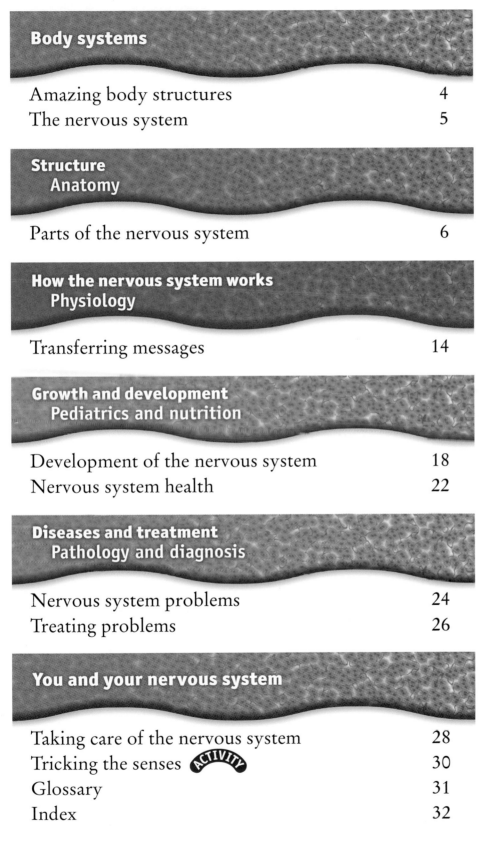

Glossary words
When a word is printed in **bold**,
you can look up its meaning
in the Glossary on page 31.

Amazing body structures

The human body is an amazing living thing. The structures of the body are divided into systems. Each system is made up of **cells**. Huge numbers of cells make up the **tissues** of the body systems. Each system performs a different, vital function. This series looks at six of the systems in the most familiar living thing to you—your body.

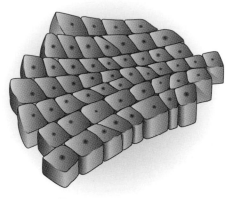

Cells make up tissues of the body systems.

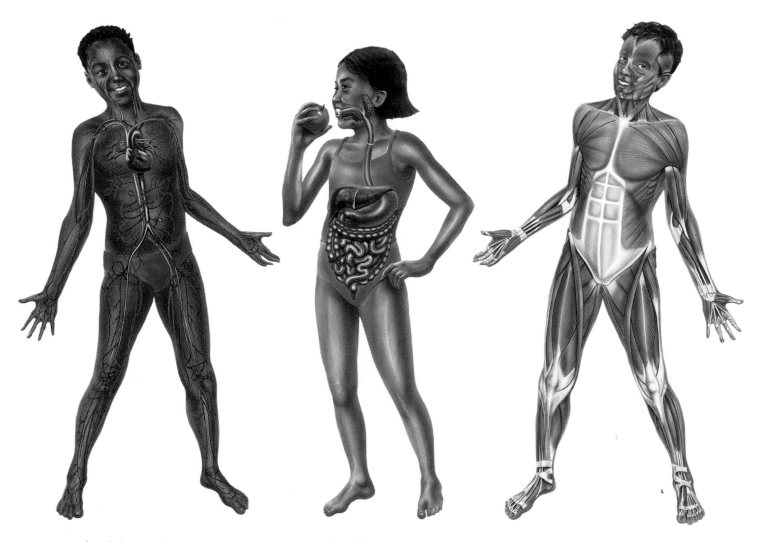

circulatory system   digestive system   muscular system

The nervous system

The nervous system is the body's control center. How much do you know about your nervous system?

- How do brain messages travel through the body?
- What do nerve cells look like?
- How do you sense the world?
- How does damage to the spine cause disability?

This book looks at the human nervous system to answer these questions and more.

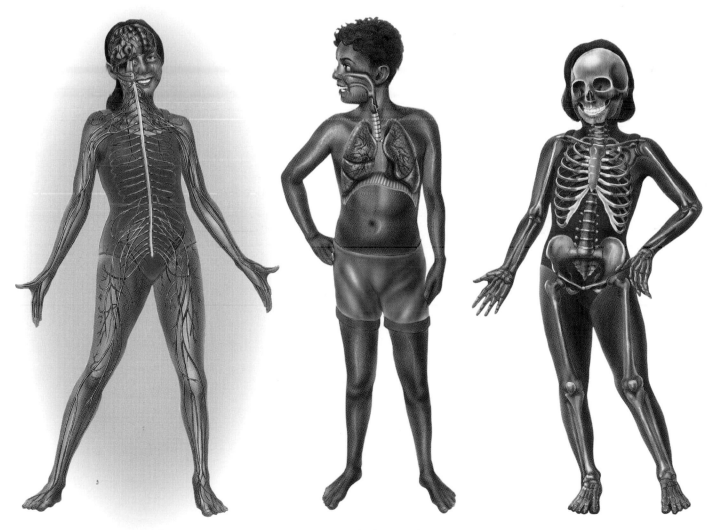

nervous system

respiratory system

skeletal system

Parts of the nervous system

The nervous system is made up of the central nervous system and the peripheral (say per-if-er-al) nervous system. Together, these two parts control the body's activities including the senses, digestion, blood circulation, and body movements. For the body to work properly all its functions need to work together. The nervous system constantly sends electrical signals through a network of nerve cells to carry out its commands.

You and your brain

Your brain is the center of your thoughts and memories. Most brain activity occurs without you even being aware of it. Your brain keeps your body functioning constantly.

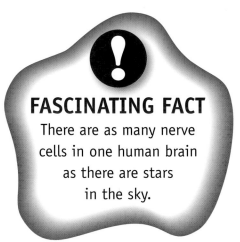

FASCINATING FACT
There are as many nerve cells in one human brain as there are stars in the sky.

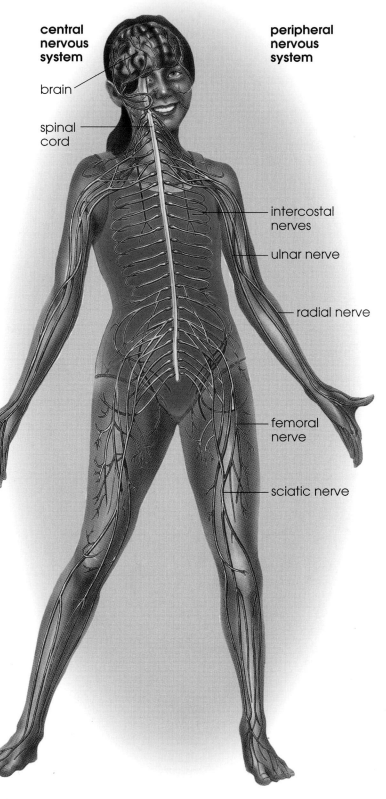

central
nervous
system

peripheral
nervous
system

brain

spinal
cord

intercostal
nerves

ulnar nerve

radial nerve

femoral
nerve

sciatic nerve

The central nervous system

The central nervous system is made up of the brain and the spinal cord. It contains around 100 billion nerve cells. Nerve cells have many extensions called **dendrites**, which connect each nerve cell to other nerve cells. **Axons** are nerve cell extensions that are much longer than dendrites. Bunches of axons combine to form nerve fibers. Nerve fibers form a network which allows nerve cells to communicate with each other.

The peripheral nervous system

The peripheral nervous system is made up of nerve fibers which extend from the central nervous system to all parts of the body. The nerve fibers transfer messages from outside the body to the central nervous system. These messages are received by the senses. The eyes, ears, tongue, nose, and skin have **receptor cells** which react to **stimuli**, such as light and sound. The peripheral nervous system also transfers messages from the central nervous system to the rest of the body. These messages tell the body what to do, such as which muscles to move.

Most nerve cells have only one or two axons and several dendrites.

Parts of the central nervous system

The brain is the main control center in the body. The spinal cord transfers messages between the brain and the peripheral nervous system.

The brain

The brain is made up of two sides of brain material, called the cerebral hemispheres. Together they make up the largest part of the brain, the cerebrum. The right cerebral hemisphere controls the left side of the body and the left cerebral hemisphere controls the right side of the body. The hemispheres communicate with each other through a band of nerve tissue called the **corpus callosum**.

Layers in the brain

There are many layers in the brain. The gray outer layer contains most of the brain's nerve cells. This layer, called the cerebral cortex, has many folds. Inside the cerebral cortex is a white layer which consists of nerve fibers formed from the axons of the nerve cells in the cerebral cortex. Deep inside the brain, under this white layer, is the **limbic system**.

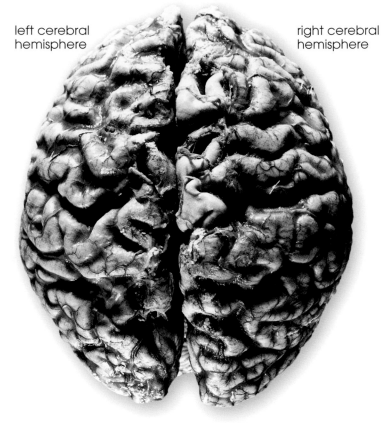

left cerebral hemisphere

right cerebral hemisphere

A human brain is divided down the middle into two halves.

TRY THIS

Hold the weight of a brain

The brain weighs about 3.3 pounds (1.5 kg). Hold a 2.2 pound (1 kg) packet of butter and a 1.1 pound (500 g) packet of butter in your hands. Close your eyes and imagine that the weight in your hands is a brain.

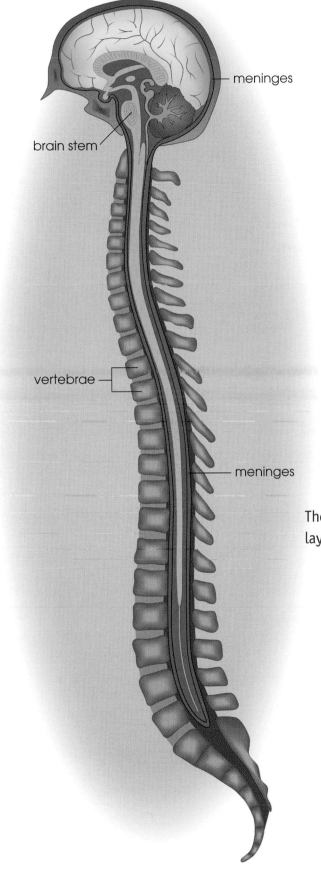

meninges

brain stem

vertebrae

meninges

The spinal cord

The spinal cord is the connecting cable between the brain and the rest of the body. It is less than 0.8 inch (2 cm) wide; about the width of one finger. Nerve fibers that come out through the **brain stem** form a cord that runs down the spine. The spinal cord is well protected by the bones in the spine, called vertebrae.

The meninges

The brain and spinal cord are wrapped in layers of tissue called the meninges (say men-in-jees), for extra protection. Between the layers of meninges is a fluid that acts like a shock absorber for the brain. This fluid stops the brain knocking on the hard skull bones and becoming damaged.

The meninges form a thin protective layer around the brain and spinal cord.

FASCINATING FACT
The disease meningitis is an infection in the meninges. The symptoms include headache, drowsiness, and flu-like symptoms.

Parts of the peripheral nervous system

Peripheral nerves come out from the spinal cord in pairs at 31 points and reach all areas of the body. There are three types of nerves in the peripheral nervous system:

- **sensory nerves**
- **motor nerves**
- **autonomic nerves.**

Sensory nerves

Sensory nerves carry incoming messages, called sensory messages, to the brain. These include messages from the skin, internal organs, muscles, and the sense organs.

Motor nerves

The motor nerves carry signals from the brain to the muscles. These signals command the muscles to move. For example, when you want to pick up a tennis ball, the brain sends a signal through the motor nerves to bend your fingers to grasp the ball.

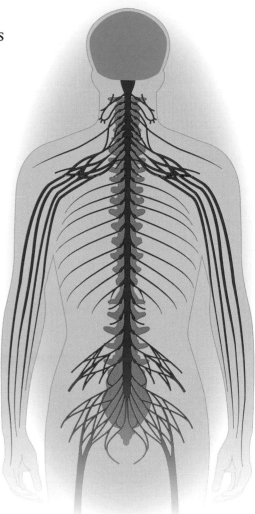

This rear view shows how the peripheral nerves extend from the central nervous system to the rest of the body.

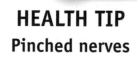

HEALTH TIP
Pinched nerves

Sometimes nerves get pinched where they come out from the spine. This causes numbness in some parts of the body.

Tip: If you have pain or numbness in any part of your body you should see a doctor.

Autonomic nerves

Autonomic nerves maintain internal body functions, such as heart beat and breathing. These actions are automatic and happen without you noticing. They occur all the time, whether you are awake or asleep. Automatic body activities are constantly monitored and adjusted by the autonomic nerves.

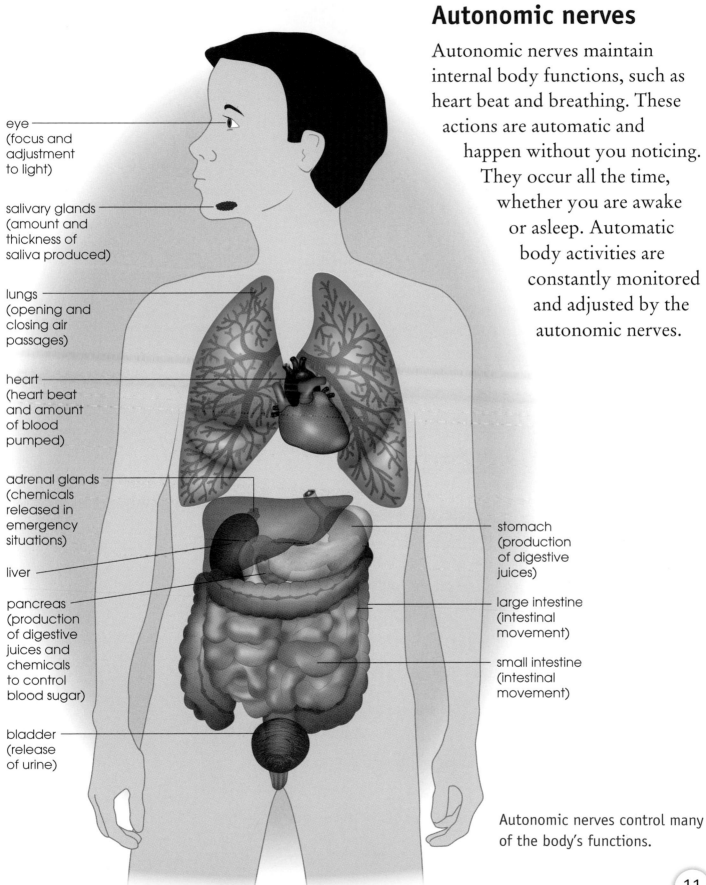

eye
(focus and adjustment to light)

salivary glands
(amount and thickness of saliva produced)

lungs
(opening and closing air passages)

heart
(heart beat and amount of blood pumped)

adrenal glands
(chemicals released in emergency situations)

liver

pancreas
(production of digestive juices and chemicals to control blood sugar)

bladder
(release of urine)

stomach
(production of digestive juices)

large intestine
(intestinal movement)

small intestine
(intestinal movement)

Autonomic nerves control many of the body's functions.

Sense organs

The sense organs receive information from outside the body. The head holds four very specialized sense organs: the eyes, ears, nose, and tongue. The skin has general sense receptors that react to touch, pressure, pain, and temperature.

Eyes

Eyes have receptor cells located at the back of the eyes. Light signals enter the eye through the cornea and pass through the eye to the receptor cells. The light signals are then converted into electrical signals. These are carried through the **optic nerve** to the brain.

**Rods and cones
UNDER THE MICROSCOPE**

There are two types of receptor cells in the eyes: rods (white) and cones (green). Rods sense shape and movement. Cones sense color.

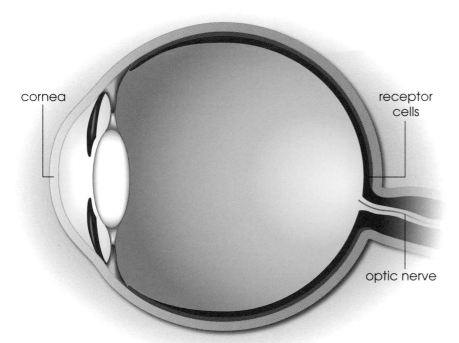

cornea

receptor cells

optic nerve

The eye is a sense organ that receives information in the form of light.

Ears

Receptor cells in the ears react to sound vibrations. Sound vibrations enter the ears and travel to the receptor cells in the inner ears. They are then converted into electrical signals and transferred to the brain through the **auditory nerve**.

The skin

The skin is the largest sense organ of the body. Nerve endings, or receptors, in the skin are sensitive to heat, touch, pressure, and pain. Some areas of the body are more sensitive than others because they have more receptors in the skin. Fingertips have more touch receptors than other parts of the body.

This area of skin may have about 200 pain receptors, a few cold receptors, 12 heat receptors, and about 20 pressure receptors.

FASCINATING FACT

Skin is made up of many structures, including hair follicles, sweat **glands**, and nerve endings. Each structure has a different function.

Transferring messages

The nervous system transfers messages to and from the brain through the body's network of nerve fibres. However, scientists do not yet fully understand how the brain works. They continue to conduct research to find out more about brain function.

Nerve cell function

When nerve cells, or neurons (say new-rons), are stimulated, an electrical signal is set off. The signal travels through the neuron and is passed along the axon to other neurons, which receive the signal through their dendrites.

Myelin covering

Some nerves are covered with a layer of fat called myelin, to help messages travel very fast. Messages in these nerves can travel at a speed of more than 0.6 mile (1 km) per second. This is 100 times faster than for nerves that do not have a myelin covering.

!

FASCINATING FACT
If you stand on something sharp, you pull your foot away in just 0.05 seconds. In this time, the pain sensors in your foot send a message to the central nervous system, which sends back a signal to move your foot.

dendrites

axon

nerve cell body

myelin covering

Neurons "fire" by passing electrical signals from one cell to the next.

Brain activity

The millions of neurons in the brain are constantly firing. Their electrical activity can be recorded on an EEG, or electroencephalogram (say e-lec-tro-en-sef-a-lo-gram). Scientists have used EEGs and brain scans, along with studies of injured brains, to map which areas of the brain are involved with different activities.

thought

movement

touch

speech

taste

hearing

vision

A map of the brain shows which areas are used for different activities.

Synapses

A synapse is a small gap between two neurons where electrical messages are transferred. This transfer is done by releasing chemicals from one neuron to the other. The chemicals, called neurotransmitters, are released by the axons and received by the dendrites. Neurotransmitters are made up of a range of chemicals, including acetylcholine, noradrenaline, serotonin, and glutamate.

Nerve cells
UNDER THE MICROSCOPE

Axons, which release neurotransmitters, are longer and thicker than dendrites.

Incoming signals

Incoming signals are collected by the senses and sent to the brain for processing.

Light

The color and intensity (brightness) of light is sensed by the rods and cones in the eye. The optic nerve then carries signals to the brain.

Sound

Receptors in the inner ear sense the pitch and volume of sound. The signals are then sent to the brain through the auditory nerve.

Chemical receptors

Receptors in the tongue and nose detect chemical signals. Tiny hairs in taste buds and in the lining of the nose trigger electrical signals that are transferred to the brain.

Heat, touch, pressure, and pain

The skin receives incoming messages of heat, touch, pressure, and pain. The messages are then transferred through peripheral nerves to the brain.

Chemical receptors in the nasal cavity detect smells in the air and send signals to the brain through the olfactory nerve.

Inner ear hair cells
UNDER THE MICROSCOPE

Tiny hair cells in the inner ear tilt when the head moves and send a message to the brain telling it what angle the head is on.

olfactory nerve

chemical receptors

nasal cavity

The endocrine system

The **endocrine system** is a control system that interacts with the nervous system. It sends chemical messages called **hormones**, which are mainly slow-acting. Thyroxine hormone controls the rate the body uses energy. Insulin controls the level of glucose in the bloodstream. Sex hormones control the development of reproductive cells. Adrenaline is a fast-acting hormone which is released during emergency situations to control reactions to emergencies.

Endocrine glands

Endocrine glands produce hormones and release them directly into the bloodstream. The pituitary gland in the skull is the most important endocrine gland because it controls other glands and stimulates growth.

Hormones work with the nervous system to control and adjust body functions.

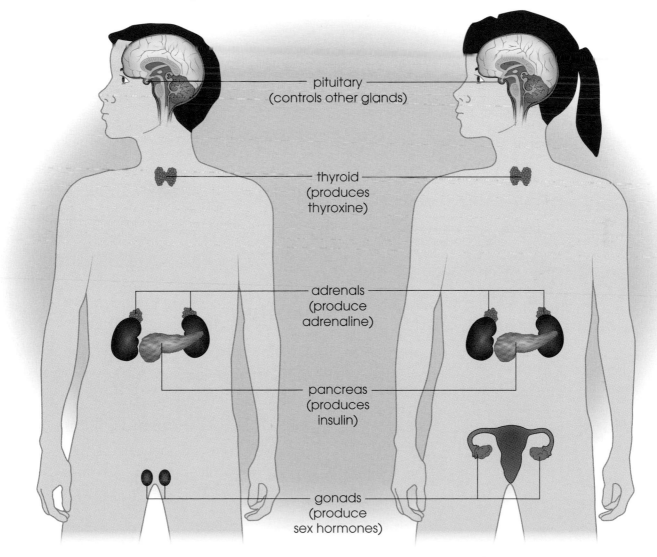

pituitary
(controls other glands)

thyroid
(produces
thyroxine)

adrenals
(produce
adrenaline)

pancreas
(produces
insulin)

gonads
(produce
sex hormones)

Development of the nervous system

At birth the nervous system is well developed, but still incomplete. Development of the nervous system continues at a fast rate in the early years of life. The number of neurons in the body does not increase once the early development stage is over.

Early development

The nervous system is among the first parts to develop in an unborn baby. Long before other body parts grow, the brain and spinal cord are well defined. Billions of links between neurons form before birth and many more are made in the years after birth.

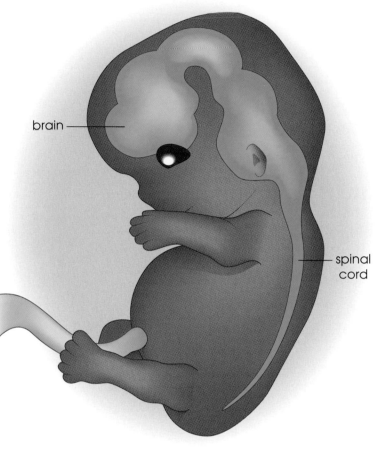

brain

spinal cord

The central nervous system develops before arms, legs, and other organs are fully developed.

FASCINATING FACT
Retrieving information that is stored in your memory involves nerve impulses traveling along pathways formed when you learned the information.

Learning

Babies are born with the ability to learn from their experiences. Learning is vital for the proper development of the nervous system. It involves neurons making new connections, not the growth of new neurons. During learning, new dendrite connections are formed and strengthened in the cerebral cortex.

Intelligence

Psychologists, scientists who study the mind, believe that people are born with a certain level of intelligence that does not change. We use our intelligence to learn, but our actual intelligence does not change. Many psychologists now think that there are different types of intelligence, such as mathematical, emotional, and social intelligence.

Intelligence tests

Intelligence is measured using tests. The first intelligence tests led to the development of measures called IQ. When these tests were developed in the 1920s, the average IQ was 100. Now the average is 105. This does not mean that people are more intelligent now than they were in the 1920s. It is more likely that people are just better at doing IQ tests.

FASCINATING FACT
Practicing IQ tests can improve your scores. This may not mean that your IQ is increasing. It may simply show that you have learned to do the tests better.

People use their intelligence to help them learn.

Memory

Memory is the brain's ability to store experiences. Various regions of the cerebral cortex appear to be involved in memory.

There are three main types of memory: sensory, short-term, and long-term. Sensory memory lasts for a few seconds and helps us in daily activities. Short-term memory can last for a few seconds or a few hours. It stores a record of recent events, such as the details of a game just played. Long-term memory is a selection of short-term memories that are stored for long periods, even for a whole life.

Thinking back to a special event involves accessing long-term memory. Memories are stored long-term if they are significant, or if they are recalled or practiced frequently after being committed to short-term memory.

HEALTH TIP
Improving memory

Mnemonics (say nem-on-iks) are methods used to help with retaining and retrieving information. They include making up rhymes to help remember things such as procedures.

Tip: Practice using rhymes to increase your memory.

Playing chess relies on short-term memory and also involves long-term memories of games played in the past.

Sense of self

Everybody has the thought and feeling of being themselves. Brain researchers are trying to identify exactly what a thought is and what makes people self-aware. Studies show that the front section of the cerebral cortex is involved in a person's sense of "being." As yet nobody really knows where "the self" is located in the brain.

Personality

Each person has a different personality, which is formed by their intelligence, creativity, set of emotions, reactions, and judgments. Personality is a combination of the thinking parts of the brain in the cortex and the emotional parts in the limbic system.

Everybody is aware of themselves and their individuality.

!

FASCINATING FACT

Psychologists study the development of babies and children to identify different stages in mental development. However, nobody knows when babies actually start to think.

Nervous system health

The nervous system, like all body systems, needs good food to remain healthy. It also needs sleep and appropriate learning experiences to develop well. Looking after the brain involves mental exercise, just as muscles need to exercise by moving.

The role of sleep

Scientists are not sure what role sleep plays, but they know that sleep is necessary for the nervous system to function properly. However, nerve cells do not rest during sleep. They carry out different activities than during waking hours. Sleep involves various stages, each involving a different pattern of brainwave activity. Scientists believe that during sleep the brain is busy making new nerve cell connections. Learning is difficult for people who suffer from lack of sleep.

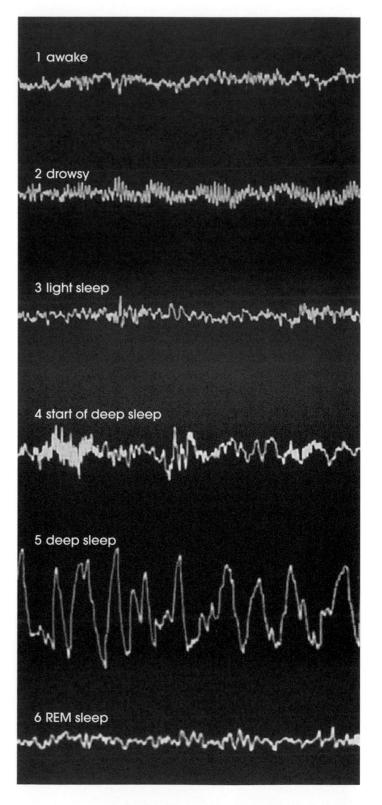

1 awake

2 drowsy

3 light sleep

4 start of deep sleep

5 deep sleep

6 REM sleep

Brainwaves are very slow in deep sleep (stage 5), but speed up again during REM sleep (stage 6), when dreaming occurs.

Chemicals in the nervous system

During times of stress the body produces chemicals called endorphins. Endorphins are like natural painkillers which reduce nerve excitement.

Drugs are chemicals that are put into the body which affect the nervous system. Stimulants such as caffeine (found in tea and coffee) increase nervous system activity. Substances such as alcohol slow down nervous system activity. Painkillers and anesthetics are drugs that reduce or "kill" pain messages sent from the brain.

Anesthetic drugs are used to dull pain during dental procedures.

HEALTH TIP
Treating headache

Headache can be treated by taking drugs, such as paracetamol, to reduce the suffering. It is important not to overuse or abuse chemicals that affect the nervous system.

Tip: If pain continues for a long time, seek medical advice.

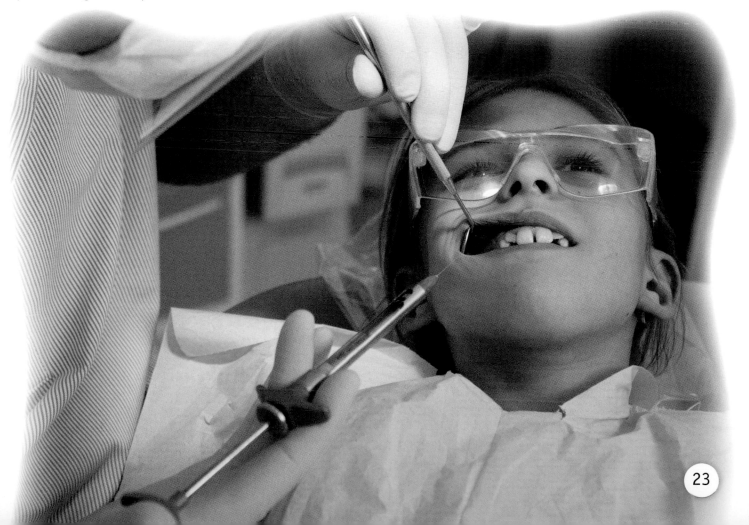

Nervous system problems

Physical injury, infections, mental disorders, and **genetic disorders** are problems that can affect the nervous system. Peripheral nerve damage leads to loss of sensation in the affected parts of the body. This damage may repair, although it can take weeks or months.

Brain injuries

Injuries to different parts of the brain affect different parts of the body. A brain injury can range from concussion (bruising of the brain), through to long-term coma (unconsciousness) and amnesia (memory loss). Hard knocks to the brain can cause nerve cells to die, leading to the permanent loss of control of some body parts. Nerve cells in the brain are not replaced when they die.

Spinal injuries

Spinal injuries can lead to paralysis, the loss of movement in some parts of the body. Damaged nerves in the spinal cord repair very slowly. Sometimes they do not repair at all. The extent of the paralysis depends on what part of the spine is injured.

FASCINATING FACT
Researchers have identified chemicals that stimulate nerves to make new dendrite connections. In the future, these chemicals may be used to repair spinal cord damage.

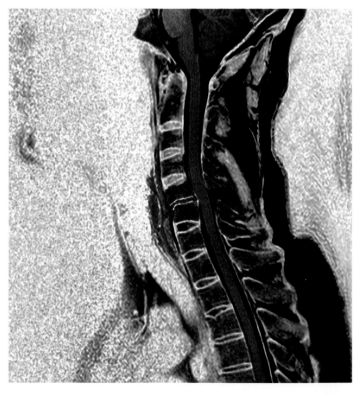

A broken neck can cause serious damage to the spinal cord.

Nerve disorders

There are many nerve disorders, or neurological problems, that people can suffer from.

Epilepsy

Epilepsy causes uncontrolled electrical activity in the brain, which can lead to loss of consciousness. Epileptic episodes, called seizures, can be small or large and quite serious.

Multiple sclerosis

Multiple sclerosis is a genetic disorder which damages the myelin covering around fast conducting nerves. This leads to problems with nerve cell function. Damaged motor nerves cause weakness and lack of control in muscles. Damage to sensory nerves causes tingling sensations and numbness.

Dementia

Dementia occurs in many people over the age of 80 years. It causes a range of symptoms, including loss of memory. One form of dementia, called Alzheimer's disease, can occur in people who are as young as 60 years old.

Leading scientist, Stephen Hawking, suffers from motor neuron disease and writes popular books with the aid of modern technology.

Motor neuron disease

Motor neuron disease is a rare condition that affects the nerves that control muscle action. The muscles controlled by these nerves become weak. The muscles involved in breathing, speaking, chewing, and using the hands are the most commonly affected parts.

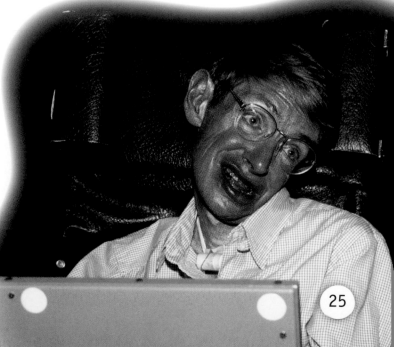

Treating problems

Nervous system problems are diagnosed using modern medical imaging techniques, such as brain scans. Medical researchers study ways to help improve the treatment of nervous system problems.

Brain scans

Brain scans can show brain structures and activity. There are various types of brain scans, including Positron Emission Tomography (PET) and Magnetic Resonance Imaging (MRI) scans, which allow the brain to be studied as it is working.

Surgery

Surgery, called neurosurgery, may be needed to rejoin nerves. Neurosurgeons use tiny instruments and microscopes to rejoin cut nerve fibers. This fine surgery requires great skill. Surgery can help patients to regain feeling and movement in their affected body parts.

During surgery, the nerves are often not connected in exactly the way they were before. This means the patient must relearn how to use the affected body parts.

A neurosurgeon uses a microscope to help carry out brain surgery.

Mental disorders

Mental disorders cause abnormal or unstable behavior, thoughts, or feelings. It is normal to experience a range of emotions in reaction to situations, such as happiness, sadness, anxiety, and depression. However, some people feel emotions that are not reactions to a situation, or can react very differently from other people in the same situation. This behavior may indicate mental illness. Many mental disorders are now being studied, but more study is needed to understand what happens in the brain during mental illness. Illnesses such as depression, schizophrenia, and bipolar mood disorder are now treated with drugs and other therapies.

FASCINATING FACT
Many teenagers suffer mood swings as the hormones in their bodies change at **puberty**. This is normal during this phase of life and should not be confused with mental illness.

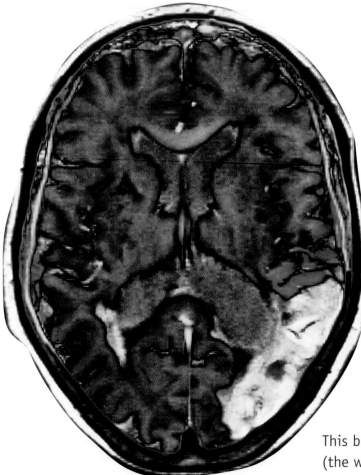

Stroke

During a stroke, blood supply to an area of the brain is restricted or cut off, which causes damage to brain cells. Brain scans can show areas that have been damaged. The loss of nerve cells in the brain leads to loss of control of associated body areas, or paralysis in one side of the body.

This brain scan shows bleeding in the brain (the white area) which caused a stroke.

Taking care of the nervous system

The nervous system is best cared for by eating good food, getting enough sleep, engaging in mental exercise, and avoiding physical injury. Many people who have suffered spinal and nerve problems are able to lead healthy, active lives.

Brain food

Eating foods containing protein is important for building brain tissue. Meat, eggs, and fish supply all the essential nutrients that the body needs to build its own proteins.

Sleep

Young people need more sleep than older people. Going to bed and getting up at the same time each day maintains a healthy sleeping pattern.

Avoiding injuries

Following safety rules can help avoid injuries. You should always:
- wear a seat belt that is correctly adjusted while traveling in a car
- wear a safety helmet when riding a bike or using a skateboard or rollerblades
- follow safety rules in gymnasiums, swimming pools, and on sports fields

People with paraplegia can participate in wheelchair sports, such as tennis.

HEALTH TIP
Alcohol and caffeine

Many drugs, such as alcohol and caffeine, affect growing brains more than adult brains. Caffeine is found in tea, coffee, and cola.

Tip: Choose drinks, such as water or juice, which do not contain caffeine.

In case of accidents

If you are nearby when an accident occurs and somebody has head or spinal injuries, remember:

- do not move the person
- if the person is conscious, ask them what parts hurt and if they can move their toes and fingers
- keep the person warm and make sure they are as comfortable as possible
- call an ambulance

Be prepared

Learn emergency service numbers and practice what to ask for (police, ambulance, or fire services). In the United States, emergency services are contacted by dialing 911.

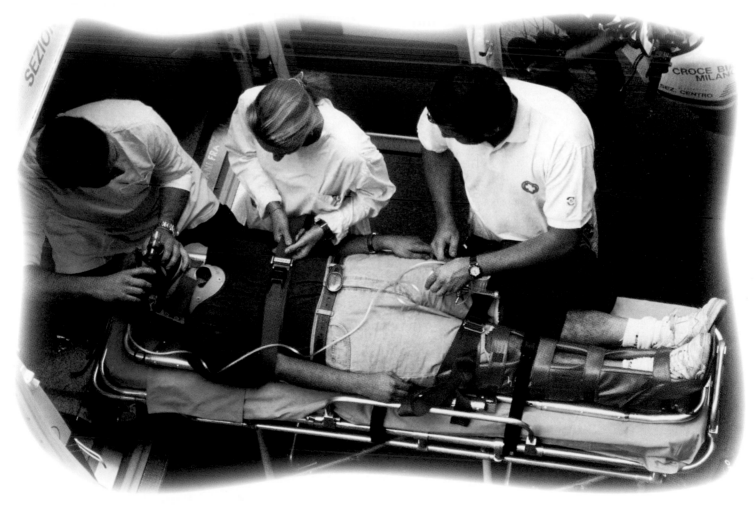

Ambulance officers put a neck brace on an accident victim to prevent spinal cord damage.

Tricking the senses

ACTIVITY

The senses tell us a great deal about the outside world, but they can be tricked. Try these activities that can trick your senses.

Optical illusions

1 Look at the picture to the right.
  What do you see?
  An old lady or a young lady?

  Explanation: Our brains
  try to make sense of what
  we see with our eyes.

2 Look at the lines to the left.
  Which line looks longer?
  Using a ruler, measure
  the length of each line,
  between the arrow heads.

  Explanation: The arrows
  pointing inwards make
  the line look longer.

Temperature illusion

Put a piece of fabric and a metal object, such as a spoon, in the freezer. They will soon be the same temperature as the freezer. Which one feels colder when you take them out and hold them both?

Explanation: The sensors in your hand are tricked into sensing the metal as colder but they are both the same temperature. The metal feels colder because the heat from your hand passes to the metal better than to the fabric.

Glossary

auditory nerve	the nerve connected to the inner ear which sends messages from the ear to the brain
autonomic nerves	nerves that control internal organs and body functions
axons	long thin extensions of nerves that carry signals to other nerve cells
brain stem	the lower part of the brain that connects to the spinal cord
cells	the smallest units of living things
corpus callosum	the part of the brain that connects the two cerebral hemispheres
dendrites	extensions of nerve cells that receive signals from other nerve cells
endocrine system	the body system which releases chemicals (hormones) into the bloodstream
genetic disorders	disorders that are inherited, or passed on in a family from one generation to the next
glands	organs that release chemicals into the body
hormones	chemical messages that are released into the bloodstream
limbic system	part of the brain that controls the emotions
motor nerves	nerves that carry messages from the brain to the muscles
optic nerve	the nerve at the back of the eye that sends messages from the eye to the brain
puberty	a stage when young people's bodies mature and become more adult
receptor cells	nerve cells that receive signals, or stimuli, from outside the body
sensory nerves	nerves that send messages to the brain
stimuli	things from outside the body, such as smells and flavors, which trigger the senses
tissues	groups of similar cells which make up the fabric of body systems

Index